Bump to Birthday®
- pregnancy and first year journal

Bump to Birthday will inspire you to capture the unique story of your pregnancy and your child's precious first year. Allow an enjoyable half an hour or so each week to complete your journal — a great opportunity to put your feet up and reflect.

A combined pregnancy and new baby journal, Bump to Birthday helps you to tell your own remarkable story and record your unique, unrepeatable experiences. The growth of your bump, your hopes and dreams, your birthing experience, and the special moments with your new baby — from first movements to first smile, first Thanksgiving, first Christmas to first birthday — will be treasured forever in one beautiful journal.

Bump to Birthday® for

DADDY

Full name …

Date of birth …

Place of birth …

Hair color …

Eye color …

Mother's name …

Father's name …

Where we met …

MOMMY

Full name …

Date of birth …

Place of birth …

Hair color …

Eye color …

Mother's name …

Father's name …

How we met …

"Before you were conceived, I wanted you.
Before you were born, I loved you.
Before you were an hour, I would die for you.
This is the miracle of a Mother's love."

Maureen Hawkins

Finding Out

FINDING OUT

Why I thought I was pregnant...

How I found out I was pregnant with you...

How I felt when I found out...

Who I told and how they reacted to the news...

Hopes and fears...

Date of last
menstrual period...

Date that you
are due to be born...

NOTES

My blood group ...

Your father's blood group ...

Ailments and mishaps I have had ...

Medication that I take ...

Family medical history ...

NOTES

My Obstetrician's name …

Address …

Contact number …

My birth partner's name …

Address …

Contact number …

The First Trimester

STAR SIGNS

ARIES
March 21st
- April 20th

TAURUS
April 21st
- May 21st

GEMINI
May 22nd
- June 21st

CANCER
June 22nd
- July 23rd

LEO
July 24th
- August 22nd

VIRGO
August 23rd
- September 22nd

LIBRA
September 23rd
- October 23rd

SCORPIO
October 24th
- November 22nd

SAGITTARIUS
November 23rd
- December 22nd

CAPRICORN
December 23rd -
January 20th

AQUARIUS
January 21st
- February 19th

PISCES
February 20th
- March 20th

THE 1st 8 WEEKS

The first day of my last menstrual period (LMP) is considered to be the first day of my pregnancy even though fertilization takes place approximately two weeks after this date.

You start off as a group of cells that divide rapidly. Your sex is already determined due to the combination of chromosomes: XX for a girl or XY for a boy.

At this stage you are called an embryo and you are C shaped. You are measured, length wise, from the top of your head to the base of your bottom – Crown to Rump Length (CRL). By the end of the 8th week you are between 0.5 and 0.9 inches CRL. *

By the end of eight weeks your heart has become the more recognisable four chambered organ, similar to mine, and your lungs have grown and divided into two main bronchi.
The right bronchus forms three secondary bronchi and three lobes and the left bronchus forms two secondary bronchi and two lobes.

Your limb buds, which are small protrusions from your body, have formed and have flattened to form your hand and foot plates. Your fingers and toes are just starting to separate. Bones and joints are starting to form.

Your eyes, which began as shallow grooves on the side of your head, now contain the developing lens, the early retina and the beginning of your optic nerve.

There are the early signs of your developing ears and nasal pits for your nose have formed. Your brain is starting to develop.

*Babies grow at different rates so all weights and measurements are averages.

WEEK 9

A bit about you...

You are now about 0.9 inches. Your skeleton is starting to turn to bone and your limbs are long and bent at the elbows and knees. Your fingers and toes are becoming defined.

Your arms have rotated by 90 degrees outwards and your legs have rotated by 90 degrees inwards, while muscles have started to develop at the base of both your arms and your legs.

Your face is starting to look more human like. Your mouth has formed and taste buds are appearing on your tongue.

A bit about me...

What we've been doing...

"It is said that the present is
pregnant with the future."

Voltaire

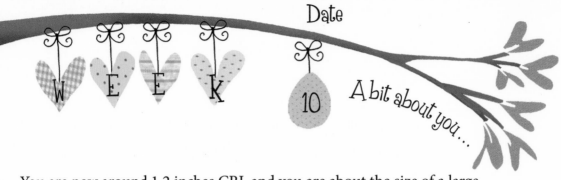

You are now around 1.2 inches CRL and you are about the size of a large grape. From this week onwards you are called a foetus.

Your body muscles are developing and you have begun moving, although feeling you at this stage is highly unlikely.

Your face continues to develop with your jaw and chin in place and the cavity between you mouth and nose are now joined.

Your ears and nose can now be seen.

Fingerprints are evident in the skin and hair follicles are beginning to form on your head and body.

A bit about me ...

Sickness ...

Feelings ...

Cravings ...

Weight ...

What we've been doing ...

Date

W E E K 11

A bit about you …

You are now around 1.6 inches CRL and weigh about 0.25 ounces.

Your fingers and toes have completely separated and can move independently. Your tooth buds, the beginning of a complete set of 20 milk teeth, are formed. You can swallow, suck and stick out your tongue.

If you are a boy, the development of your genitalia is dependent on your testicles producing a form of the hormone testosterone. If you are a girl the development of your female genitalia is promoted by estrogen and other hormones in my body.

The placenta, the organ that allows oxygen and nutrient exchange between us, changes to deal with your increased demands and the amount of amniotic fluid increases.

A bit about me...

What we've been doing...

"Being a mother means
that your heart is
no longer yours; it
wanders wherever your
children do."

unknown

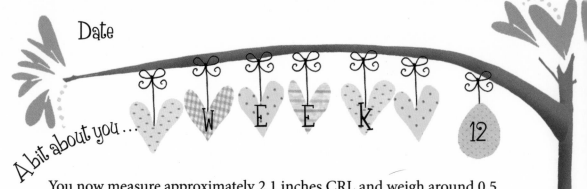

A bit about you...

WEEK 12

You now measure approximately 2.1 inches CRL and weigh around 0.5 ounces. You are about the size of a plum.

Most of your major organs are formed and your kidneys have started to function. You have a facial profile and eyelids cover your eyes. These will remain shut to protect your delicate eyes until about the seventh month of pregnancy. Your vocal chords are developed and you can, and do, sometimes cry out.

Your brain is forming and you can feel pain. Hair is beginning to form on your head and your fingers and toes have both developed soft nails.

A bit about me...

Sickness...

Feelings...

Cravings...

Weight...

What we've been doing...

SONOGRAMS

Who was there...

WEEK 13

You are now about 2.9 inches CRL and weigh around 0.8 ounces. You are starting to look like a proper baby as you start to make facial expressions.

By the end of this week you will be fully formed and your sex could be discovered.

The umbilical cord contains two arteries and one vein. An elastic connective tissue called wharton's jelly protects the umbilical vessels from possible mechanical pressure and creasing.

Your blood group is determined and may not be the same as mine.

What we've been doing…

The Second Trimester

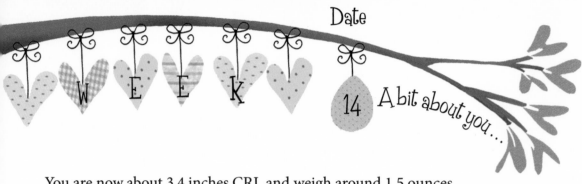

You are now about 3.4 inches CRL and weigh around 1.5 ounces.
You are approximately the size of a lemon.

Your eyes are slowly moving towards the centre of your face and your nose is more pronounced. Your external ears are fully formed and are now in the correct position on the sides of your head. Your heart is beating about twice as fast as an adult – around 140 beats per minute. Your kidneys have started to produce urine.

The first body hair, a fine downy hair called lanugo hair, is appearing. Your cheek bones are visible.

If you are a girl then your ovaries are moving downwards towards your pelvis whilst, if you are a boy, your prostate gland is developing.

A bit about me...

Sickness...

Feelings...

Cravings...

Weight...

What we've been doing...

Date

WEEK 15

A bit about you...

You are now about 4 inches CRL and weigh around 2.5 ounces.

Your body has now grown longer than your head and your legs have grown longer than your arms – so you are now more in proportion.

You are getting heavier, not only as you grow, but due to the development of the bones within your skeletal system which are hardening.

Your transluscent skin is all covered by lanugo hair. This is usually shed around birth and replaced by coarser hair.

A bit about me...

What we've been doing...

"Children reinvent your world for you."

Susan Sarandon

WEEK 16

You are now about 4.6 inches CRL and weigh around 3.5 ounces. You are approximately the size of an avocado.

Your fingers and toes are now fully formed and you can grasp. You will be moving your limbs about as you kick and somersault around as there is currently lots of room. More developed facial muscles mean that you have more defined facial expressions such as frowning.

Your breathing motion is evident at this stage and can be seen as regular chest movements, inhaling and exhaling small amounts of amniotic fluid. These actions help the lungs to grow and develop in preparation for breathing air after your birth.

Sickness...

Feelings...

Cravings...

Weight...

What we've been doing...

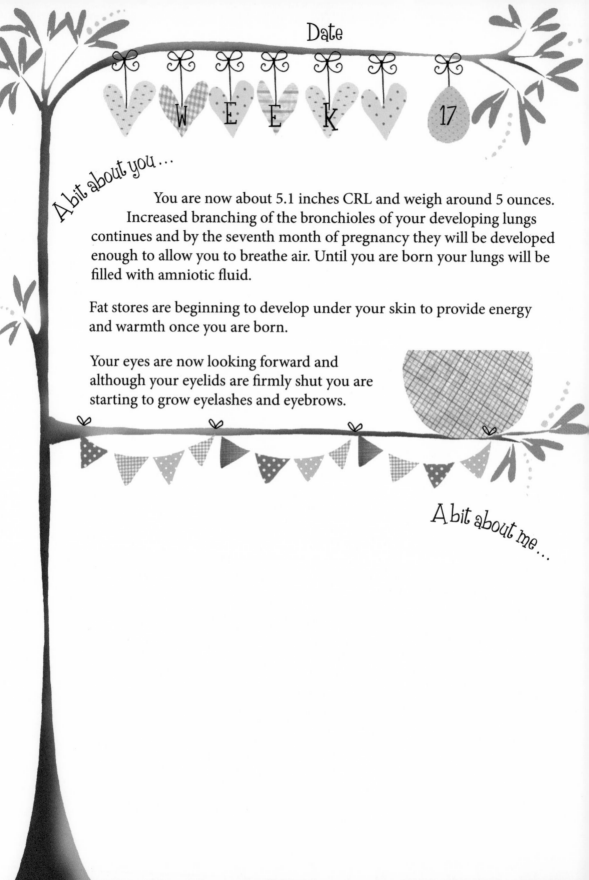

Date

WEEK 17

A bit about you...

You are now about 5.1 inches CRL and weigh around 5 ounces. Increased branching of the bronchioles of your developing lungs continues and by the seventh month of pregnancy they will be developed enough to allow you to breathe air. Until you are born your lungs will be filled with amniotic fluid.

Fat stores are beginning to develop under your skin to provide energy and warmth once you are born.

Your eyes are now looking forward and although your eyelids are firmly shut you are starting to grow eyelashes and eyebrows.

A bit about me...

What we've been doing…

"Making a decision to have a child – it's
momentous. It is to decide forever to
have your heart go walking around
outside your body."

Elizabeth Stone

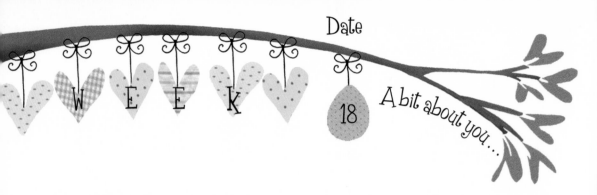

You are now about 5.6 inches CRL and weigh around 6.7 ounces. You are approximately the size of a medium sweet potato.

Meconium, which is made up of digestive products and swallowed amniotic fluid, starts to accumulate in your bowel. This black sticky substance will be your first bowel movement.

You are covered with a whitish paste-like protective material called vernix, it protects the skin against the softening actions of the amniotic fluid.

You will be starting to develop regular sleep and awake patterns and you may have a favorite sleep position.

A bit about me ...

Sickness ...

Feelings ...

Cravings ...

Weight ...

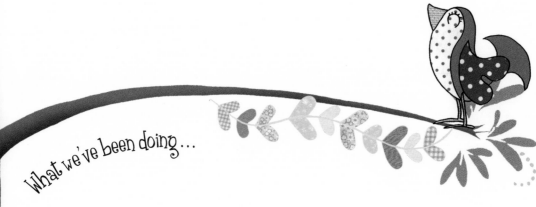

What we've been doing ...

WEEK 19

A bit about you …

You are about 6 inches CRL and weigh around 8.5 ounces.

Your facial features are now distinct and your scalp hair, which may not yet be visible on your head, continues to grow.

Your nervous system is developing rapidly as nerve fibres start to become coated with myelin, which is essential for the proper functioning of the nervous system.

If you are a girl your uterus and fallopian tubes are in place. Girls are born with a finite number of eggs and at this stage you will have approximately six million. If you are a boy your genitals are distinct and recognisable and you will be able to generate new sperm throughout your life. A sonogram can now determine if you are a boy or a girl.

A bit about me...

What we've been doing...

"Everything grows rounder and wider and weirder, and I sit here in the middle of it all and wonder who in the world you will turn out to be."

Carrie Fisher

Date

You are about 6.5 inches CRL and weigh around 10.5 ounces.

This is an important time for sensory development. Specialised areas of the brain are forming to help you to interpret the nerve impulses it will receive from your senses: taste, smell, hearing, sight and touch.

You have recognisable ear structures. From now, until when hearing becomes functional at around 25 weeks, nerves will grow to allow your ears to communicate with your brain.

The sebaceous glands in your skin continue to make the oily substance vernix which, as well protecting the skin from the amniotic fluid, has antimicrobial properties important for skin surface defence.

A bit about me ...

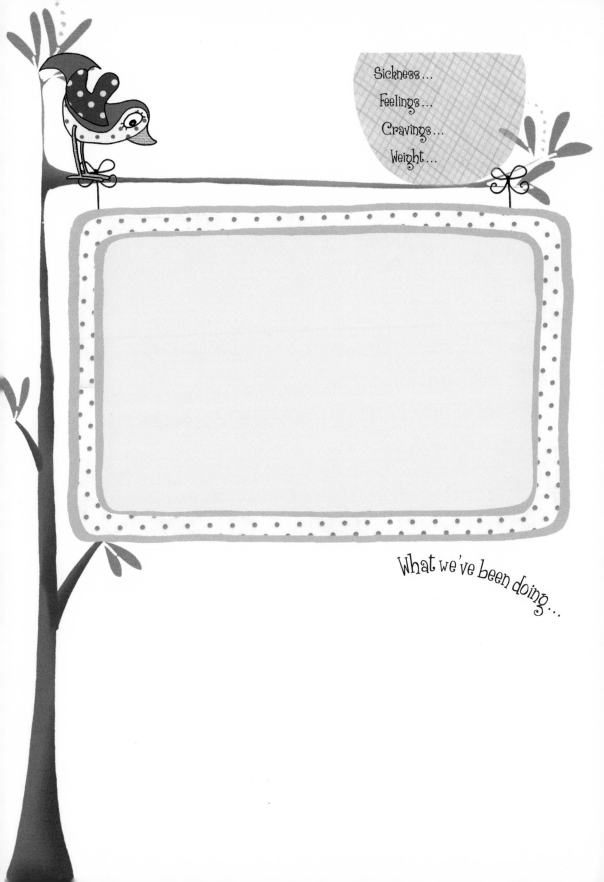

Sickness...

Feelings...

Cravings...

Weight...

What we've been doing...

Date

SONOGRAMS

Who was there...

How I feel...

WEEK 21

A bit about you…

You are now measured heel to crown. You are about 10.2 inches long and weigh around 12.7 ounces.

Your bone marrow has started making blood cells, a job done by the liver and spleen until this point. The placenta has provided nearly all of your nourishment, however now you will begin to absorb small amounts of sugar from swallowed amniotic fluid.

Your skin is thickening and becoming opaque. You are steadily gaining fat and the vernix is now a thick, waxy coat which will ease your delivery.

A bit about me…

What we've been doing...

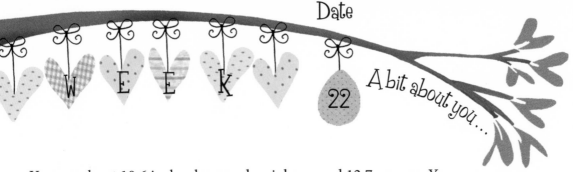
You are about 10.6 inches long and weigh around 12.7 ounces. You are approximately the size of a papaya.

Your eyebrows and eyelids are fully developed and you have fingernails. Your eyelids are shut and although the iris of your eye is formed it still lacks the pigment that will determine your eventual eye color. Your skin is thickening, but it is still very thin and wrinkly and will not smooth out until you start to deposit lots of fat during the third trimester.

Taste buds are forming on your tongue. Although your teeth are unlikely to appear until you are at least six months old, calcification of your incisor and canine teeth begins in the tooth buds beneath your gums.

A bit about me …

Sickness …

Feelings …

Cravings …

Weight …

What we've been doing …

Date

WEEK 23

A bit about you…

You are now about 11.3 inches long and weigh around 1.1 pounds.

The bones located in the middle ear have hardened and your fully developed inner ear means you have a sense of whether you are upside down or right side up in my womb.

Your skin pigment is now forming and your eyebrows are visible. You are now proportioned like a newborn except you are a thinner version since your baby fat has not developed much yet.

Your pancreas, essential in the production of hormones, continues to develop and you have begun to produce insulin, important for the breakdown of sugars.

A bit about me...

What we've been doing...

"Think of stretch marks
as pregnancy service
stripes."

Joyce Armor

BEFORE YOU ARE
BORN I WOULD
LIKE TO ...

ADVICE I HAVE
BEEN GIVEN...

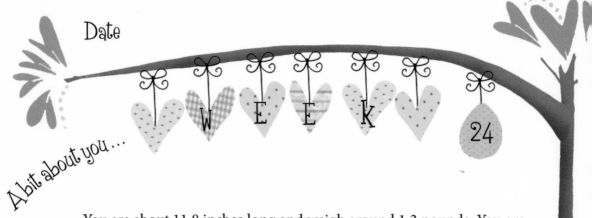

WEEK 24

A bit about you...

You are about 11.8 inches long and weigh around 1.3 pounds. You are gaining approximately 0.2 pounds per week. This weight gain is in muscle, bone mass and organs.

Your lungs now start producing specialised cells within their small branches that produce surfactant. This is an important substance which helps to prevent the air sacs in your lungs from collapsing when you start to breathe air at birth.

Taste buds continue to develop on your tongue, which is fully formed. If I drink something strange or bitter you will probably be able to tell.

Little creases have appeared on the palms of your hands and the soles of your feet. The muscular co-ordination of your hands and mouth has improved as you suck your fingers, hands and even your feet. Over the next few weeks sweat glands will be forming in your skin.

A bit about me...

Sickness...

Feelings...

Cravings...

Weight...

What we've been doing...

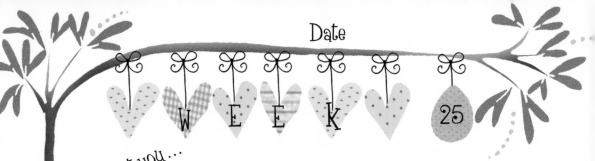

WEEK 25

A bit about you...

You are about 13.6 inches long and weigh around 1.5 pounds You are now pretty well built proportion wise even though you still have little body fat and your skin is thin. The structures of your spine are forming – all 33 vertebra, 150 joints and 1000 ligaments.

Your tiny brain is growing rapidly and your auditory system is complete so that you can hear sounds. Your hands are fully developed and, although some of the nerve connections to the hands have a long way to go, dexterity is improving. You will be able to touch your hand to your face, and one hand to another or clasp your feet.

Your nostrils begin to open and the nerves around your mouth and lip area are more sensitive. Your swallowing reflexes are also developing.

A bit about me...

What we've been doing...

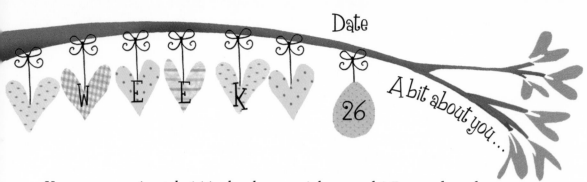

You are approximately 14 inches long, weigh around 1.7 pounds and you are about the size of an aubergine. Your little feet are about 2 inches long.

You can hear so you will be able to hear my heartbeat, my stomach rumbling or blood flowing through the umbilical chord. A loud noise will produce changes in amniotic function which can affect your heart rate and blood pressure.

Your brain continues to grow with increasing brain wave activity for the visual and auditory systems.

Your hands are active and muscle coordination is such that you can easily get a thumb into your mouth. Sucking motions help to strengthen your cheek and jaw muscles. A fetal brain scan would show that you can respond to touch.

A bit about me…

Sickness…

Feelings…

Cravings…

Weight…

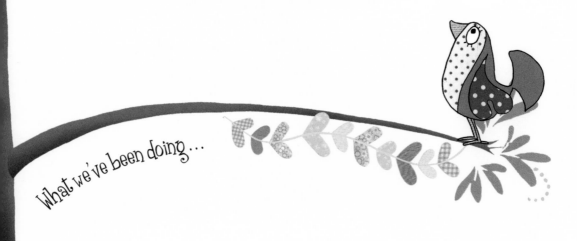

What we've been doing…

Date

WEEK 27

A bit about you…

You are about 14.4 inches long and weigh around 1.9 pounds. Your head is over 2.7 inches in diameter. You now have eyebrows and eyelashes and your hair is growing every day. Your muscle tone is improving and your body is getting plumper.

The iris now has pigment within it, although your final eye color will not be determined until some months after you are born. You can open your eyes, but mostly you will keep them shut.

As the auditory system becomes more developed you continue to become familiar with everyday sounds including voices and music.

Your little body is covered in vernix so you look like a long distance swimmer.

A bit about me...

What we've been doing...

"The most important thing she'd learnt over the years was that there was no way to be a perfect mother and a million ways to be a good one."

Jill Churchill

The Third Trimester

Date

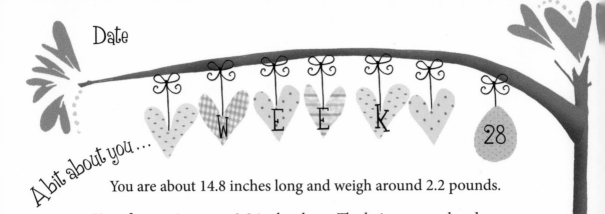

WEEK 28

A bit about you...

You are about 14.8 inches long and weigh around 2.2 pounds.

Your feet are just over 2.2 inches long. The hair on your head may now be visible. Little milk teeth have developed under your gums.

From now on you will put on lots of body fat and your muscles will become more toned. During the next few weeks, while there is still room to move around, you are likely to be at your most active.

The nerve connections from your ears to your brain are complete and you are beginning to recognise and react to sounds such as language and music.

A bit about me...

Sickness…

Feelings…

Cravings…

Weight…

What we've been doing…

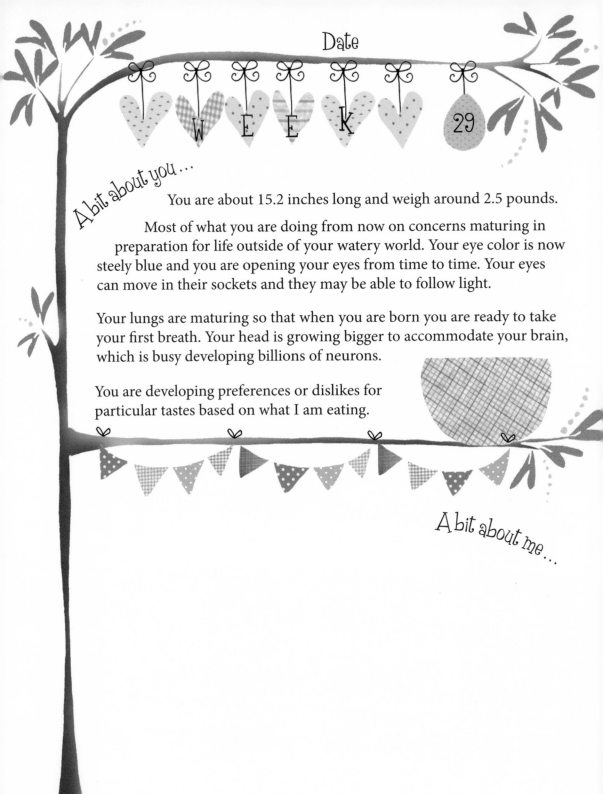

Date

WEEK 29

A bit about you…

You are about 15.2 inches long and weigh around 2.5 pounds.

Most of what you are doing from now on concerns maturing in preparation for life outside of your watery world. Your eye color is now steely blue and you are opening your eyes from time to time. Your eyes can move in their sockets and they may be able to follow light.

Your lungs are maturing so that when you are born you are ready to take your first breath. Your head is growing bigger to accommodate your brain, which is busy developing billions of neurons.

You are developing preferences or dislikes for particular tastes based on what I am eating.

A bit about me…

What we've been doing...

"There is no friendship, no love, like
that of a mother for her child."

Henry Ward Beecher

You are about 15.7 inches long and weigh around 2.9 pounds. You are approximately the size of a small melon.

For several months the umbilical cord has been your lifeline. Nourishment is transferred from my blood through the placenta and into the umbilical cord to you. From now on your own bone marrow is responsible for red cell production. The red blood cells will continue to service your body by transporting oxygen and removing waste products.

You have begun storing iron, calcium and phosphorus as well as fat so that you will be able to control your body temperature.

Your head and body are now proportioned like a newborn. Your eyelids are opening and closing more regularly and they are sensitive to light.

A bit about me …

Sickness …

Feelings …

Cravings …

Weight …

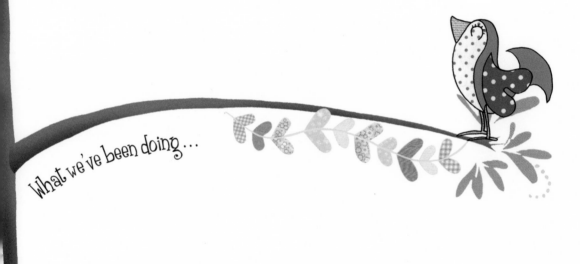

What we've been doing …

Where I would like to give birth ...

MY BIRTH
PREFERENCES

Who else do I want to be present at my labor ...

Things I would like to take with me ...

How I would like my baby to be monitored during the labor and birth ...

Preferred positions for labor and birth...

My thoughts on pain relief...

How I would like to feed my baby...

How I feel about assisted delivery...

Date

W E E K 31

A bit about you ...

You are about 16.2 inches long and weigh around 3.3 pounds.

Almost all of your major body organs are functioning, your growth will focus on maturing those organs and growing muscle mass and fat stores.

Your lungs and digestive tracts are very near to being mature and over the next few weeks your lungs will continue to develop so that you can breath when you are born.

As you grow the amount of amniotic fluid decreases. There is currently about a pint and a half surrounding you.

From now on, your weight gain will exceed your growth lengthwise.

A bit about me...

What we've been doing...

"The only thing worth
stealing is a kiss from
a sleeping child."

Joe Houldsworth

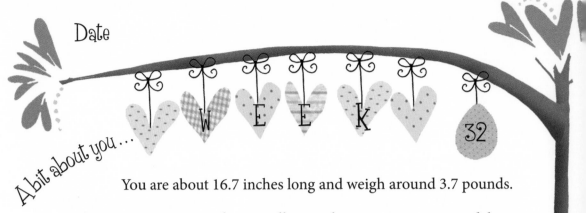

A bit about you...

You are about 16.7 inches long and weigh around 3.7 pounds.

The uterus is getting to be a small space for you to move around, but there is enough room to swish about. You will be turning your head from side to side and moving your hands and feet.

The amniotic fluid helps to protect your head and cushion it against any trauma while the brain is developing. The diameter of your head is almost 10cm, but the skull bones remain unfused to allow you to be born more easily.

During the next few weeks about half of my weight gain will go directly to you.

A bit about me ...

Sickness...

Feelings...

Cravings...

Weight...

What we've been doing...

WEEK 33

You are about 17.2 inches long and weigh around 4.2 pounds.

You are using your lungs to practise breathing by inhaling amniotic fluid and you may regularly have hiccups. You drink about a pint of amniotic fluid a day now and you are urinating about the same amount.

The early baby fuzz, lanugo, is disappearing and is being replaced by coarser body hair. Your nails are long enough to reach the tip of your fingers and toes so you could scratch your face before you are born.

What we've been doing…

"There are three reasons for breast-feeding: the milk is always at the right temperature; it comes in attractive containers; and the cat can't get at it."

Irena Chalmers

You are about 17.7 inches long and weigh around 4.7 pounds. You are approximately the size of a honeydew melon.

Your skull bones are still pretty flexible and not completely joined. This is to help to ease the exit out of the narrow birth canal.

Fat accumulations plump up the arms and the legs this week. Your skin is also becoming less wrinkled.

Thanks to antibodies crossing from me, through the placenta to you, you are developing immunities to mild infections.

Your sleep patterns are now the same as they will be when you are born. Your eyes are open when you are awake and closed when you are asleep.

A bit about me …

Sickness …

Feelings …

Cravings …

Weight …

What we've been doing …

What I am least looking forward to...

LOOKING FORWARD
TO THE BIRTH

What I am most looking forward to...

Date

WEEK 35

A bit about you...

You are about 18.2 inches long and weigh around 5.3 pounds.

Your fat stores will help you regulate your body temperature after you are born. Although you still don't have enough fat deposits beneath your skin to keep warm outside my womb, you are putting it on fast.

Your lungs are almost fully developed. Your reflexes are more coordinated, you turn your head, grasp firmly and respond to sounds, light and touch.

A bit about me...

What we've been doing...

"Babies are always more
trouble than you thought -
and more wonderful."

Charles Osgood

Date

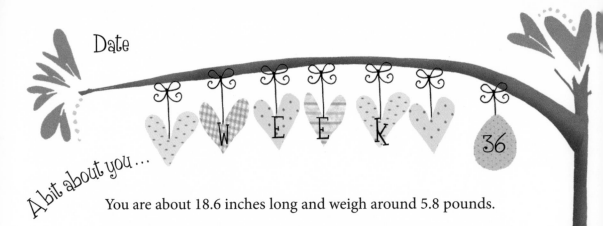

WEEK 36

A bit about you...

You are about 18.6 inches long and weigh around 5.8 pounds.

In general, babies gain about 8 to 9 ounces per week from now until birth. As you continue to gain weight, fat deposits are forming and you will be getting creases and folds around your neck, thighs, wrists and ankles.

You will probably have started descending into the lower part of my uterus, into the pelvis, and whatever position you are in now is likely to be the position you will be in for the birth.

A bit about me...

Sickness...

Feelings...

Cravings...

Weight...

What we've been doing...

WEEK 37

A bit about you...

You are about 19.1 inches long, weigh around 6.3 pounds and you are approximately the size of a melon. You are growing rapidly now.

You are now considered to be 'full term' and you could be born at any time. You are taking up lots of room now and you will be curled up with your knees bent up and your arms tucked in.

You are practising breathing, sucking and swallowing amniotic fluid and generally preparing to be born.

A bit about me...

What we've been doing…

You are about 19.6 inches long and weigh around 6.8 pounds.

Your main job now is to gain weight. You continue to lay down fat stores that will help regulate your body temperature after birth. Your wrinkled skin is becoming baby smooth. The amount of amniotic fluid has reduced.

You may have a full head of hair now, although it may be no more than a peachy fuzz. Most of the downy coat of lanugo that covered you for weeks has gone, although there may be some on the upper back and shoulders when you arrive.

The vernix has nearly gone and, as it is shed into the amniotic fluid, you will be swallowing it along with the lanugo hair and other secretions. These will become your first bowel movements, a blackish waste called meconium.

A bit about me …

Sickness …

Feelings …

Cravings …

Weight …

What we've been doing …

Date

WEEK 39

A bit about you...

You are about 20 inches long and weigh around 7.2 pounds.

Some of the fat you are depositing is called brown fat and it will be up to 5% of your body weight when you are born. It is mainly stored at the nape of your neck. Its primary function is to generate body heat as when you are first born you will not be able to shiver to help you generate warmth. It is called brown fat because it contains iron which makes it look brown.

The bones of your skull are able to slide over each other so that they overlap, allowing your head to pass through the birth canal without being damaged. Your joints and ligaments are flexible so that your body can twist and turn during your birth.

A bit about me...

What we've been doing...

"Mommy is such a lovely name. In the park when it is called every mother's head turns with protective anticipation."

Helen Stephens

Date

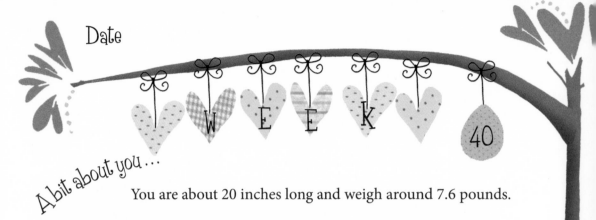

WEEK 40

You are about 20 inches long and weigh around 7.6 pounds.

You have reached the point where all of your organs and body systems are functioning and you are ready to enter the world.

Approximately 15% of your body is composed of fat and 65% of you is composed of water.

Breast buds appear in both sexes. Your genitalia will be enlarged and swollen due mainly to extra fluid in your body, but also due to a few maternal hormones. Your eyes may also be a bit puffy.

A bit about me…

Sickness...

Feelings...

Cravings...

Weight...

What we've been doing...

Date

WEEK 40+

Only 5% of babies arrive on their due date and, if you aren't with me yet, you are officially overdue!

You are preparing for the birth and putting on weight.

Without your protective vernix coat, your skin may be a little dry and flaky as you lie for some extra time in the amniotic fluid.

A bit about me...

What we've been doing…

Sickness…

Feelings…

Cravings…

Weight…

BABY SHOWER

Who organized the baby shower ...

Where it was held ...

When it was held ...

Who came ...

GIFTS

NOTES

SYMPTOMS

Pregnancy symptoms I have had…

The Birth

L A B O R

My labor
started at …

on …

at …

How I knew I was in labor …

How I felt …

What helped during my labor…

My biggest surprise on being in labor…

I was in labor for…

THE BIRTH

Description of the birth…

Who cut the cord…

Who dressed you…

My first words to you...

First outfit...

Who cried...

YOUR BIRTHDAY

Date of birth …

Time of birth …

Day of birth …

Place of birth …

Weight …

Length …

Head circumference …

Hair color …

Blood group …

Who you look like …

Your name & why you were given it …

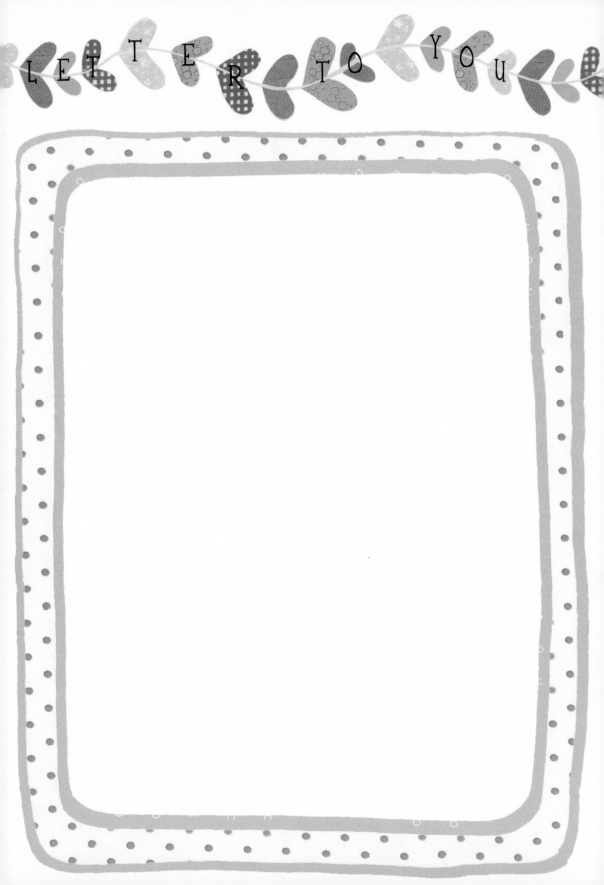

LETTER TO YOU

YOU ARE HERE

How I am feeling now you are here ...

How I feel not being pregnant ...

Who I spoke to first about your arrival ...

LETTER TO ME

ON THIS DAY

World news...

Sports news...

Celebrity news...

Weather...

Best selling books…

Popular music…

Movies that are showing…

Price of a few items…

The First Month

We went home at   on

HOME SWEET HOME

What you were wearing…

Your first home…

FRIENDLY FACES

Your first visitors were...

Date

1st WEEK

A bit about you...

A bit about me...

What we've been doing…

"A baby is born with a need to be
loved – and never outgrows it."

Frank A Clark

2nd WEEK

Date

A bit about you...

A bit about me …

What we've been doing …

Date

3rd W E E K

A bit about you...

A bit about me…

What we've been doing…

"Babies are such a nice
way to start people."

Don Herold

Date

4th **WEEK**

A bit about you...

A bit about me...

What we've been doing...

GROWING UP

Age	Weight	Height
1 month		
2 months		
3 months		
4 months		
5 months		
6 months		
7 months		
8 months		
9 months		
10 months		
11 months		
12 months		

A Few Firsts

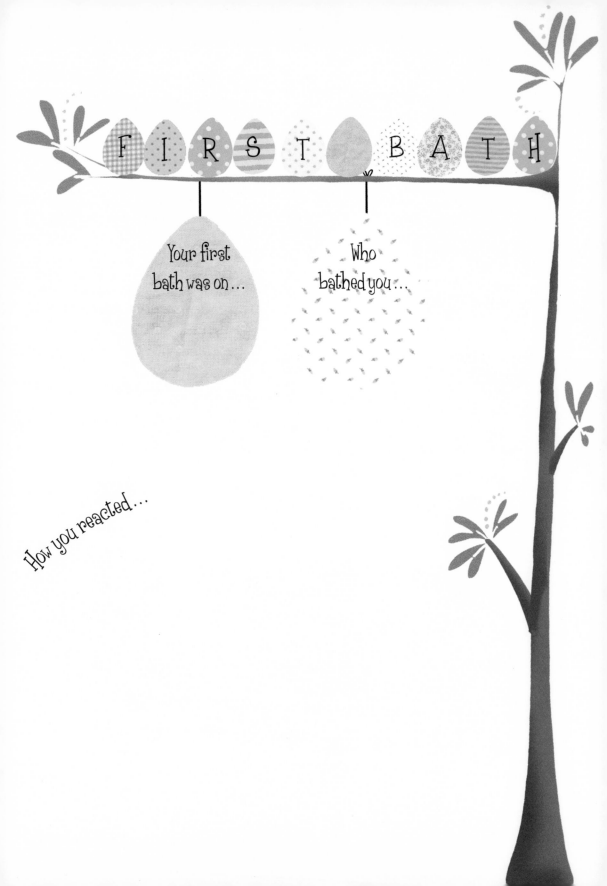

FIRST BATH

Your first
bath was on ...

Who
bathed you ...

How you reacted ...

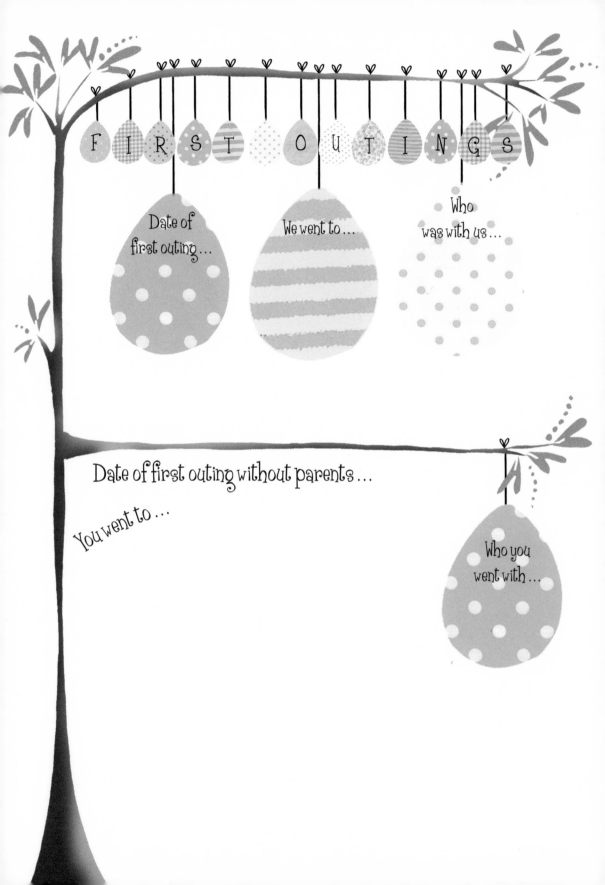

FIRST OUTINGS

Date of first outing …

We went to …

Who was with us …

Date of first outing without parents …

You went to …

Who you went with …

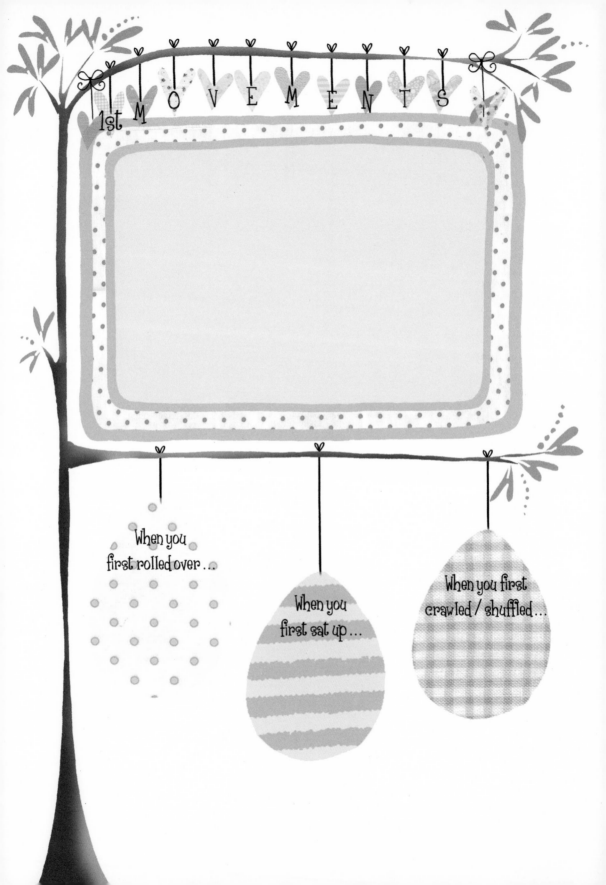

1st MOVEMENTS

When you
first rolled over...

When you
first sat up...

When you first
crawled / shuffled...

When you
first cruised…

When you
first stood up…

When you
first walked…

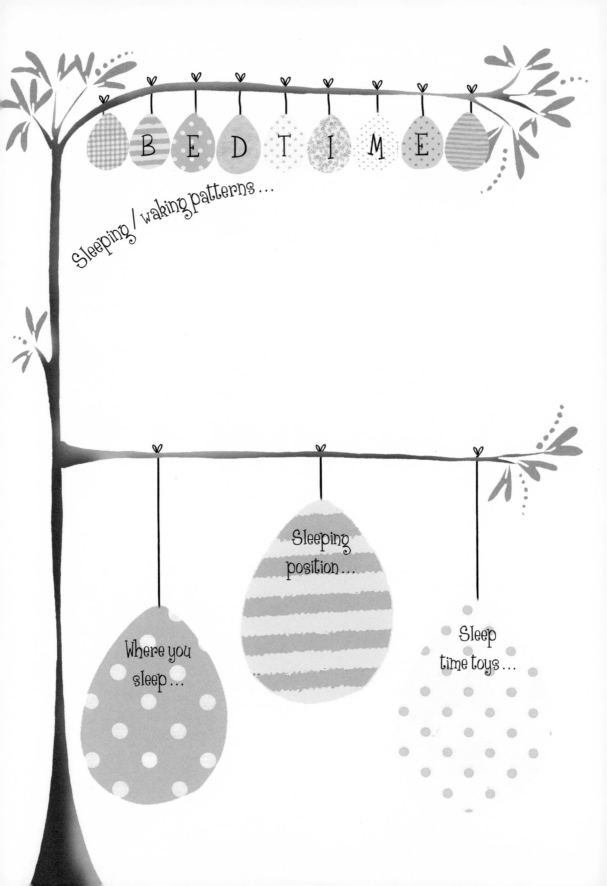

BEDTIME

Sleeping / waking patterns…

Where you sleep…

Sleeping position…

Sleep time toys…

FEEDING

Feeding patterns…

First ate solid food…

First drank from a cup…

First ate puréed food…

First ate finger food…

How you were fed…

Favorite foods…

FIRST LEFT
FOOTPRINT

FIRST RIGHT
FOOTPRINT

Who was there . . .

THANKSGIVING

What we did for your first Thanksgiving . . .

Where we were...

1st W O R D S

Favorite songs and rhymes...

Your first
sounds...

Your first
word...

Your first
sentence...

Favorite books…

What you
called Daddy…

What you
called Mommy…

What you
called yourself…

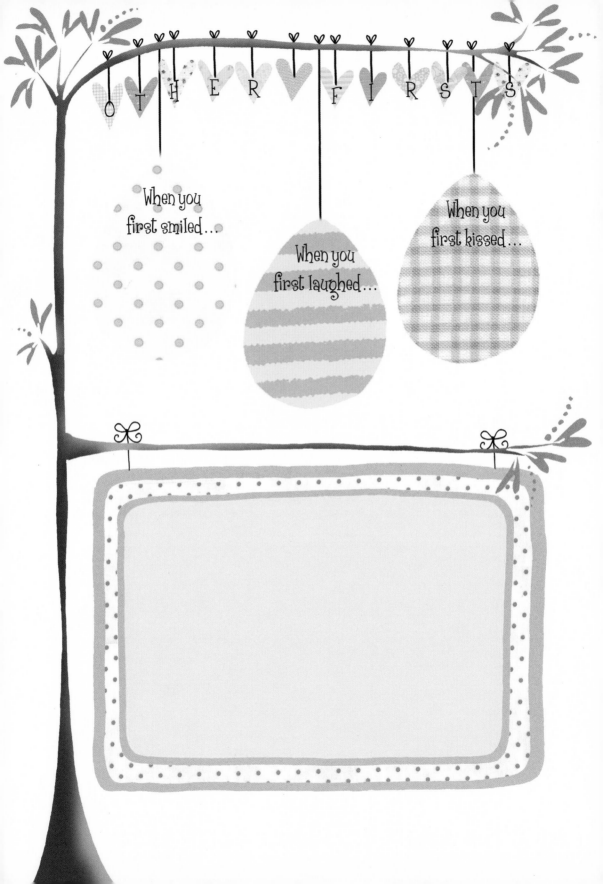

OTHER ♥ FIRSTS

When you
first smiled…

When you
first laughed…

When you
first kissed…

When you
cut your first
tooth …

When you
got your first
shoes …

When you
had your first
haircut …

Who
was there…

Where
we stayed…

What
you ate for
dinner…

FIRST CHRISTMAS

What we did…

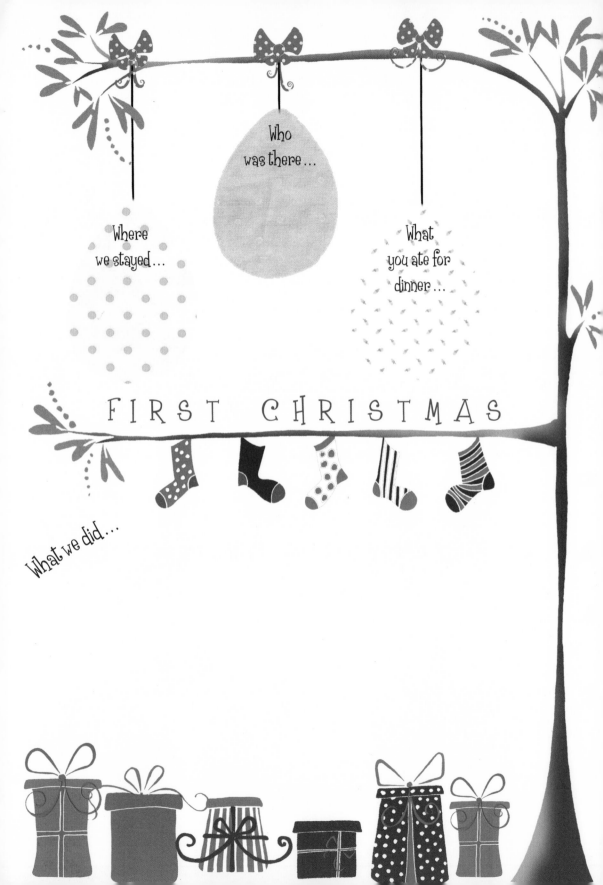

A few of your gifts…

FIRST VACATION

When
we went ...

You were ...

months old

How
we got there ...

Where we went...

Some of your adventures...

Who was there …

FIRST BIRTHDAY

What we did for your first birthday…

Some of your gifts…

Your cake…

What you wore . . .

"There are two lasting bequests we can
hope to give our children.
One of those is roots, the other is wings."

Hodding Carter

NOW YOU ARE 1

Bump to Birthday®

Bump to Birthday first published by Journals Of A Lifetime, an imprint of from you to me ltd, in January 2012. USA edition April 2013.

5 7 9 11 13 15 14 12 10 8 6 4

ISBN 978–1–907048–48–7

Author and creative by Helen Stephens.

Designed and published in the UK.

Printed and bound in China by Imago. This paper is manufactured from pulp sourced from forests that are legally and sustainably managed.

Every effort has been made to credit all quoted material correctly; should there be any omissions in this respect we apologise and shall be pleased to make the appropriate changes in any future edition.

from you to me
The Old Brewery
Newtown
Bradford on Avon
BA15 1NF, UK

hello@fromyoutome.com
www.JournalsOfALifetime.com

Published by *from you to me*

For a full range of all our titles where journals & books can also be personalized, please visit

www.JournalsOfALifetime.com